Odile Bailloeul

Celebration
Transfers for
Embroidery

SEARCH PRESS

First published in Great Britain 2010 by Search Press Limited,
Wellwood, North Farm Road, Tunbridge Wells, Kent TN2 3DR

Published in France 2010 as Transferts de Fête by
Le Temps Apprivoisé (LTA). 7, rue des Canettes, 75006, Paris

Copyright © 2010, LTA, a division of Meta-Éditions

English translation by Cicero Translations

English translation copyright ©
Search Press Limited 2010

English edition edited and typeset by
GreenGate Publishing Services

ISBN: 978-1-84448-507-9

Graphic design: Coline de Graaff
Layout: Coline de Graaff
Embroidery: Hélène Le Berre
Items made by: Géraldine Boilley-Hautbois,
Louise Martinez
Photoengraving: Alesia Studio

Contents

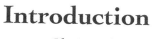

Introduction

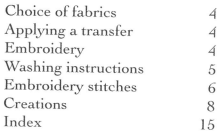

Transfer motifs

Introduction

Whether you are already an expert or are just taking your first steps in embroidery, you will find some useful ideas here for motifs to transfer and embroider on to your fabrics. You can reproduce them exactly as you see them here or use them as inspiration for making new creations.
Here you will find a range of suggestions in different styles. Motifs can be used on their own to decorate children's clothing or table napkins, for example, or can be incorporated into more complex compositions, such as decorating tablecloths, cushions or curtains.

Choice of fabrics

N.B. The fabric should not be too dark as the transfer outlines must still be visible once they have been applied.
Cotton or linen fabric are preferable, as they are easier to work with than silk or velvet.
Fabrics printed with a fairly light design can also be used for your embroidery.

Applying a transfer

1. Cut out your chosen transfer motif, leaving a small margin around the design.
2. Decide where you are going to put the motif on your fabric. If you want to place several motifs over a larger area, mark the positions with tailor's chalk or a non-permanent marker pen.
3. Place a piece of paper over your ironing board to protect it – sometimes the transfer passes through the fabric and risks marking the board. Set your iron to 'wool' and do not use steam.
4. Place the fabric on the ironing board, right side up. Place the cut-out transfer motif on to the fabric with the printed side of the transfer face down on the fabric. Attach it with some adhesive tape or pins.
5. Iron carefully with small movements to prevent the fabric from moving.
6. Check that the print has been transferred successfully by lifting one edge. If not, iron it again.

Tip
One transfer can be used three to eight times, depending on the thickness of the fabric. If used carefully, it can even be reproduced a dozen times on normal cloth.

Embroidery

Use an embroidery frame or hoop – you will achieve a better finish more easily. Do not place the frame of the hoop in the middle of an embroidered design as it could damage it. For a successful result, the embroidery design should be contained entirely within the hoop.

Duplicating motifs:

If you want to use a motif several times, but are afraid that after a while it will no longer transfer, use a sheet of carbon paper to transfer your patterns on to the fabric – this is also available for dark fabrics. Place it under your cut-out motif and trace over the motif with a pencil.

Inverting motifs:

The tracing paper is transparent enough for you to be able to see the motif on the back. If you want to reproduce a motif by inverting it, you will need to proceed using carbon paper as indicated above after turning your design over.

Using motifs:

Feel free to use different bases – as well as tablecloths or place mats, you can embroider clothes and accessories, for example babies' nightwear, gift bags, glasses cases, the cover of a photo album, etc. Use these ideas to create a range of beautiful, personalised gifts.

Combining motifs:

These themes can be combined in different ways by using them as angles, borders and central motifs. But you can also mix the themes themselves – feel free to put calves with Easter chicks and sheep for a countryside theme, or birthday sweets with Christmas gingerbread for a gourmet theme. Just let your imagination do the work.

Washing instructions

If you have embroidered your motif on cotton or linen, you can wash it in warm, soapy water. Your embroidery will be safe in a washing machine if you put it into a wash bag or pillowcase beforehand.

Once it has been washed, iron the embroidered fabric on the reverse, placing the embroidery on a piece of flannelette to prevent it being flattened.

Here are some examples of combined motifs.

Christmas tablecloth
(transfers pages 28, 36, 40)

Valentine's Day
(transfers pages 53, 56, 61)

Have a go!
This publication is dedicated to special occasions. Feel free to have a go at more ambitious projects, such as a large tablecloth for birthdays that you can get out each time it's another member of your family's turn to blow out candles – add a set of initials for each person's birthday. It will be a nice memory for everyone …

Embroidery stitches

Running stitch
Sew from right to left, with the needle passing alternately under and over the fabric.

Straight stitch
This long backstitch is used on its own or grouped together, sometimes in different directions.

Stem stitch
This is a backstitch, sewn from right to left or from left to right. The needle pierces the middle of the previous stitch, without crossing the thread, and always on the same side of it (either above or below the stitches).

Backstitch
This is a regular backstitch, sewn from right to left going back into the hole where the needle previously came out.

Chain stitch
Sew from top to bottom or from right to left. Bring the needle through to the right side of the fabric. Go back into the hole where the needle came out; pull it through to the reverse, retaining a loop of thread. The needle comes out again in the middle of the loop before going back through the same hole.

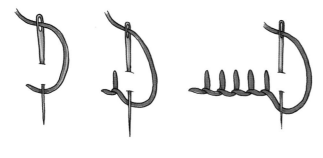

Blanket stitch

This stitch is sewn from left to right. The needle goes into the fabric and comes out vertically. Pass the thread under the needle, holding it in place with the left thumb. Pull and repeat.

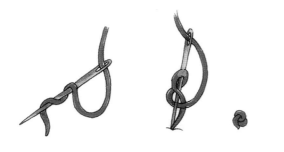

French knot

Bring the needle through to the right side of the fabric. Make a flat loop with the thread – pass the needle through the middle of the loop, going back into the hole where the needle came out.

Padded satin stitch

Before sewing this stitch, which is similar to satin stitch, embroider a series of running stitches to pad out the embroidery and give it some depth.

Satin stitch

These are regular, parallel straight stitches, worked close to one another, that can adapt to any type of surface.

Long-and-short stitch

This is embroidered like satin stitch, but with alternate long and short stitches.

Creations

HAPPY EASTER

Stitches used:
  Satin stitch (two strands)
  Long-and-short stitch (two strands)
  Stem stitch (two strands)
  Backstitch (two strands)

Threads used:
  DMC stranded cotton thread
  Three colours: dark pink (3350), light pink (3733)
  and yellow (3078)

Transfers pages 108, 112, 113, 117, 121, 125

TO THE HAPPY COUPLE

Stitches used:
Satin stitch (two strands)
Long-and-short stitch (two strands)
Stem stitch (two strands)
Backstitch (one brin)

Threads used:
DMC stranded cotton thread
Six colours: white (B5200), dark blue (930), light blue (3752), dark pink (223), light pink (3727) and brownish pink (632)

Transfers pages 41, 49, 52, 53

▼

A NEW BABY

Stitches used:
Satin stitch (two strands)
Long-and-short stitch (two strands)
Backstitch (two strands)

Threads used:
DMC stranded cotton thread
Four colours: brown (3031), dark blue (926), light blue (927) and pale yellow (745)

Transfers pages 85, 88, 89, 92

▲

HAPPY BIRTHDAY

Stitches used:
  Satin stitch (two strands)
  Long-and-short stitch
  (two strands)
  Stem stitch (two strands)
  Backstitch (two strands)

Threads used:
  DMC stranded cotton thread
  Two colours: pink (893) and red (817)

Transfers pages 128, 129, 132, 141

▼

YOU AND ME

Stitches used:
  Stem stitch (two strands)

Threads used:
  DMC stranded cotton thread
  One colour: white

Transfers pages 72, 76   ▶

HALLOWEEN

Stitches used:

Satin stitch (two strands)

Long-and-short stitch (two strands)

Stem stitch (one or two strands)

Threads used:

DMC stranded cotton thread

Five colours: black (310), pale yellow (727),

orange (742), violet (333) and green (166)

Transfers page 68, 69, 76

FINE CROWN

Stitches used:

Satin stitch (two strands)

Stem stitch (three strands)

Threads used:

DMC stranded cotton thread

Two colours: pink (915) and green (3819)

Transfers pages 44, 65 ▶

▼

HAPPY BIRTHDAY

Stitches used:

Satin stitch (two strands)
Long-and-short stitch (two strands)
Stem stitch (one or two strands)
Straight stitch (three strands)

Threads used:

DMC stranded cotton thread
Seven colours: blue grey (927), sky blue (3761),
mauve (210), pink (3805), orange (3854),
yellow (445) and green (954)

Transfers pages 132, 133

Index

Designs

CHRISTMAS EMBROIDERY

Stitches used:

- Satin stitch (two strands)
- Long-and-short stitch (two strands)
- Straight stitch (two strands)
- French knot (two strands)
- Backstitch (three strands)

Threads used:

- DMC stranded cotton thread
- Two colours: white and sky blue (747)

Transfers pages 17, 28, 29, 32

JOYEUX
NOEL

Merry
Christmas

Feliz navidad

BUON

NATALE

NOEL

Gioie

Weihnachten

Vive les mariés!

Liebe

¡Vivan los novios!

Viva gli sposi!

Amour

Valentine's day

Herbst

Halloween

AUTOMNE

El otoño

l'automne

Herbst

Halloween

AUTOMNE

El otoño

L'autunno

Baby

benvenuto

a bambino

welcome

to baby

Bambino

Baby

Welcome
to baby

Bambino

Spring

Frühling

Happy

easter!

Printemps

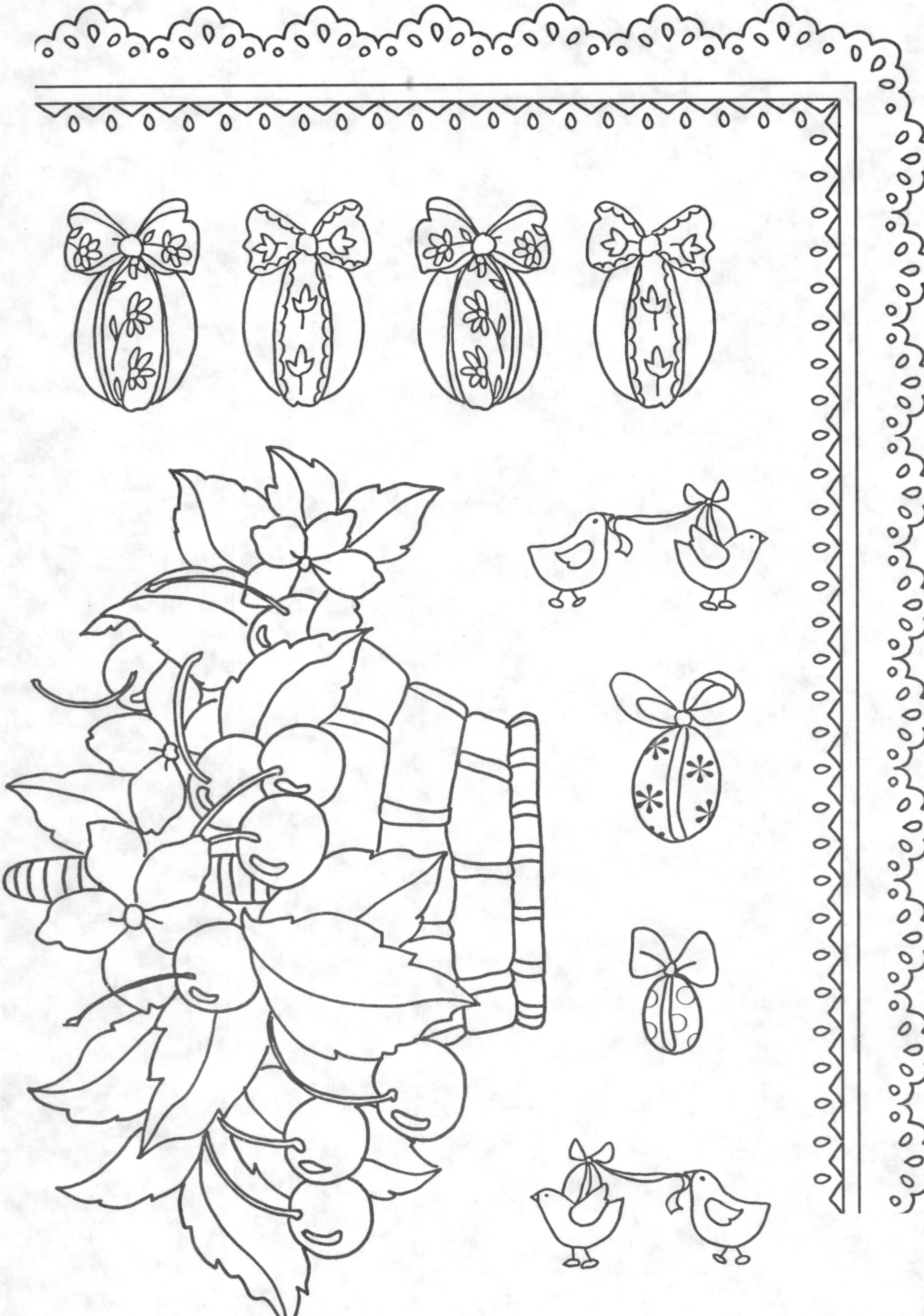

BUONA PASQUA

HAppy

Birthday

Joyeux

Anniversaire

Fröhliches

Geburstag

Happy Birthday

Joyeux Anniversaire

Fröhliches Geburstag

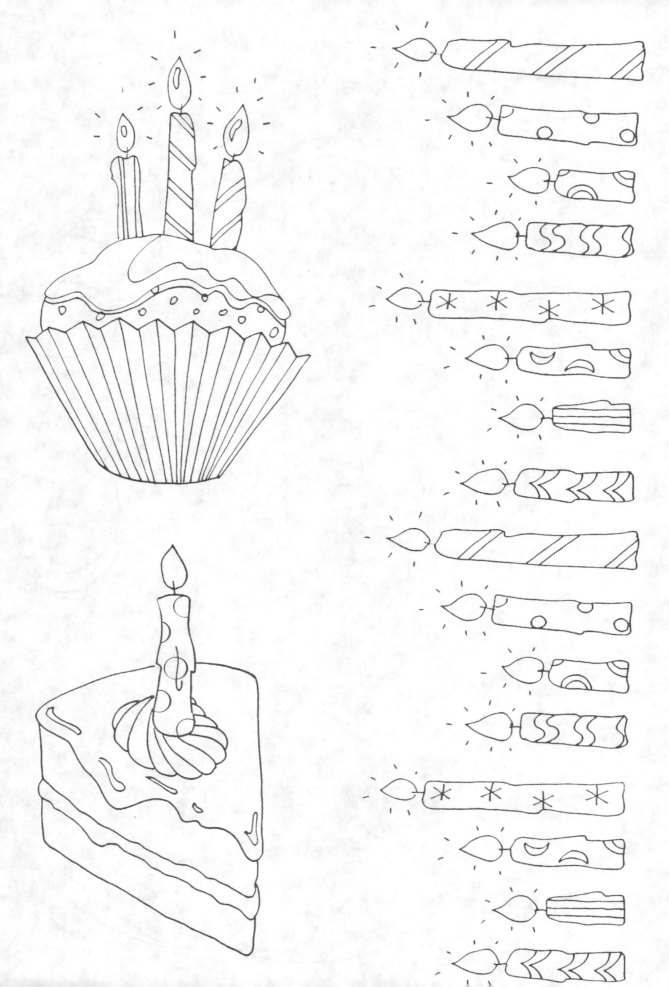

JoYEUX
ANNiVERSAiRe!

Bonne
Fête

AUGTURH